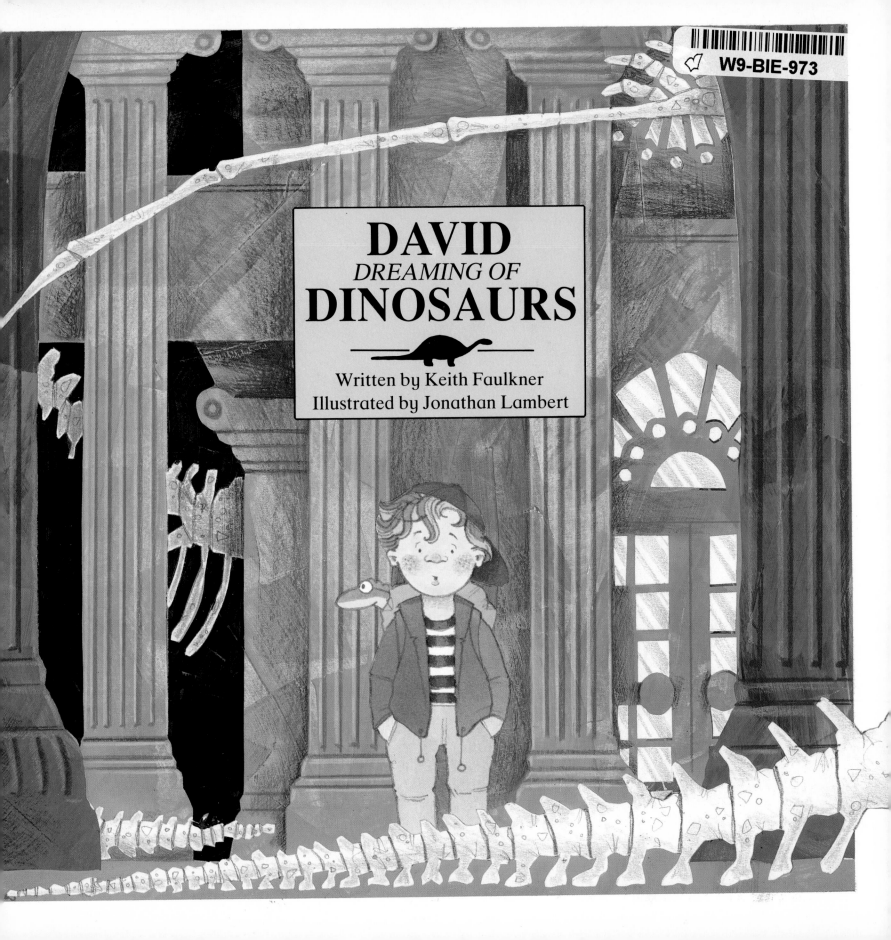

DAVID
DREAMING OF
DINOSAURS

Written by Keith Faulkner
Illustrated by Jonathan Lambert

Hi! My name's David. I'm crazy about dinosaurs . . . I'd visit this museum every day if I could.

I always dream of what these creatures must have looked like when they were alive . . . long, long ago. Wow!

TYRANNOSAURUS
ty-RAN-o-saur-us

The dinosaur all folks have seen,
The monster of the movie screen.
This creature's starred in many thrillers,
The king of prehistoric killers.

He was the Earth's most fearsome thing.
Tyrannosaurus – Tyrant King.
Beside a monster big as that.
A lion would be a pussy cat.

He lived in times we call Cretaceous.
His appetite, it was voracious.
If he were still alive today
I think I'd stay inside and play!

I know the name of almost every dinosaur. But, here's my favorite, the huge apatosaurus . . . it's bigger than our school bus!

Gosh, look at its giant bones. Imagine it alive . . . stomping through the swamp . . . Awesome!

Climb the stairs . . . walk the long corridors. Mmm, I'm hungry.

Time for lunch. This is the perfect place, underneath the huge wing of a giant pteranodon.

APATOSAURUS
ah-PAT-o-saur-us

150 million years ago.
Give or take a year or so.
Apatosaurus roamed around
And left its footprints in the ground.

This giant sauropod was strong
And grew to 65 feet long.
Not much else that came before us
Was bigger than Apatosaurus.

Deep in the ground lay its great bones,
Until time turned them into stones.
But now you can all come and see 'em.
They're on display at your museum.

Ah! Here's iguanodon. What's that picture on the wall? I guess it's how they thought it looked in 1853 . . . They put a horny spike on its nose instead of its thumb! . . . Huh! Dumb!

Someday, if I work real hard in school . . . I can get a job at a museum and go looking for dinosaur bones.

Iguanodon 1853

PTERANODON (*Pterosaur*)
tayr-AN-o-don

Just think of all the things you'd see,
If you lived in prehistory.
You'd see some wonderous creatures there.
Both on the ground and in the air.

The one sight that I most wish for,
To see a flying Pterosaur.
They must have been amazing things.
Soaring up high on leathery wings.

It's such a shame no human eyes,
Have seen them gliding through the skies.
I search the air, but all in vain.
We'll never see their like again.

IGUANODON
ig-WAHN-o-don

When people started digging bones,
Long ages had turned them into stones.
They really had no idea whether
These bones they found would fit together.

A million bones lay scattered around.
Like broken jigsaws on the ground.
But no one there had ever seen
The shape these creatures must have been.

They pondered very hard upon,
The bones of Iguanodon.
They found some horns, and I suppose,
Thought they came from the creature's nose.

P.S. We now know this idea was dumb.
The spike was really on its thumb.

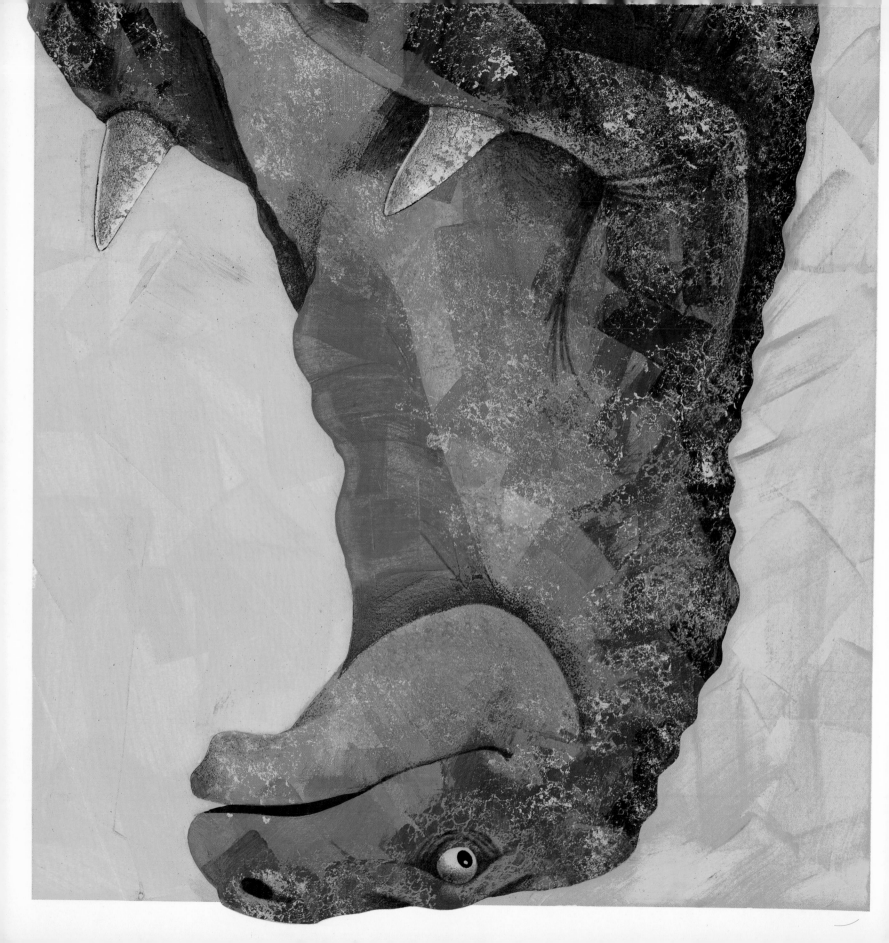

What's this? . . . Don't remember seeing this glass case before. Who's this little guy in here? Comp...sog...nathus.

Hey! This little dinosaur was no bigger than a chicken! It would make a great pet!

COMPSOGNATHUS
komp-SOG-nath-us

Most people who don't know enough
Think all dinosaurs were big and tough.
The truth is very strange to tell,
For some of them were small, as well.

One creature that lived way back then,
Was hardly bigger than a hen.
If Compsognathus you should see,
It wouldn't even reach your knee.

So when you dream about the past,
Don't think all dinosaurs were vast.
Though some were giants, this is true.
A lot were small, like me and you.

Home again . . . My own room . . .
I've got a great collection of
dinosaurs. But, it's not like the
real thing . . .

If only I was born two hundred
million years ago . . .